Expanding Vocabulary Through KJV Bible Verses

Book 1

This book is dedicated to God, to the current generation of children, to future generations, and to my own children (Aurora, Mercy, Linkin, and Gracie).

ISBN-10:   0989486508
ISBN-13:   978-0-9894865-0-7

Dear Parents and/or Educators,

This book contains 180 short lessons, one for each day of the school year. It includes Bible, vocabulary, writing, and copywork. If you would like to include Bible verse memorization, you may have you child memorize each week's verse.

This is a stand-alone workbook. There is no teacher's guide. The instructions are straight forward and easy to understand. You may modify the lessons if you wish.

The weeks are not divided into chapters, as the additional pages required for that would have meant more paper, thus increasing both the cost of production and the sales price. Instead, the lessons flow smoothly in order, one right after the other. This is also beneficial for weeks when schoolng is done for fewer than 5 consecutive days, whether it be due to personal choice, sickness, holidays, or some other reason. This makes it easy to just pick up right where you left off without feeling that you're behind on your lessons. If you don't want to switch vocabulary words mid-week though, feel free to double up on lessons until you're at your desired place in the book.

I hope this book gives your child a better understanding of biblical language and that it is a blessing to you, your child, and all those whose lives you impact.

Happy learning, and God bless!

Sincerely, Randi

Expanding Vocabulary Through KJV Bible Verses

Book 1

Then let them take a young bullock with his meat offering, even fine flour mingled with oil, and another young bullock shalt thou take for a sin offering.

- Numbers 8:8

mingled

mingled: mixed with

Write the word **mingled** on the line below.

_____

Then let them take a young bullock with his meat offering, even fine flour mingled with oil, and another young bullock shalt thou take for a sin offering.

- Numbers 8:8

mingled

mingled: mixed with

Write the word **mingled** on each line below.

_____

_____

_____

Then let them take a young bullock with his meat offering, even fine flour mingled with oil, and another young bullock shalt thou take for a sin offering.

- Numbers 8:8

mingled

<u>mingled</u>: mixed with

Write the word **mingled** and its meaning on the lines below.

_____

_____

_____

_____

_____

Then let them take a young bullock with his meat offering, even fine flour mingled with oil, and another young bullock shalt thou take for a sin offering.

- Numbers 8:8

mingled

mingled: mixed with

Write the Bible verse from above (Numbers 8:8) on the lines below.

_____

_____

_____

_____

_____

_____

Then let them take a young bullock with his meat offering, even fine flour mingled with oil, and another young bullock shalt thou take for a sin offering.

- Numbers 8:8

mingled

mingled: mixed with

On the lines below, write your own sentence using the word **mingled**.

_____

_____

_____

_____

_____

Rejoice in the Lord always: and again I say, Rejoice.

- Philippians 4:4

rejoice

<u>rejoice</u>: to be glad and joyful

Write the word **rejoice** on the line below.

_____

Rejoice in the Lord always: and again I say, Rejoice.

- Philippians 4:4

rejoice

<u>rejoice</u>: to be glad and joyful

Write the word **rejoice** on each line below.

_____

_____

_____

Rejoice in the Lord always: and again I say, Rejoice.

- Philippians 4:4

rejoice

rejoice: to be glad and joyful

Write the word **rejoice** and its meaning on the lines below.

_____

_____

_____

_____

_____

_____

Rejoice in the Lord always: and again I say, Rejoice.

- Philippians 4:4

rejoice

rejoice: to be glad and joyful

Write the Bible verse from above (Philippians 4:4) on the lines below.

_____

_____

_____

_____

_____

Rejoice in the Lord always: and again I say, Rejoice.

- Philippians 4:4

rejoice

<u>rejoice</u>: to be glad and joyful

On the lines below, write your own sentence using the word **rejoice**.

_____

_____

_____

_____

_____

_____

While the earth remaineth, seedtime and harvest, and cold and heat, and summer and winter, and day and night shall not cease.

- Genesis 8:22

cease

cease: stop, end

Write the word **cease** on the line below.

_____

While the earth remaineth, seedtime and harvest, and cold and heat, and summer and winter, and day and night shall not cease.

- Genesis 8:22

cease

cease: stop, end

Write the word **cease** on each line below.

_____

_____

_____

While the earth remaineth, seedtime and harvest, and cold and heat, and summer and winter, and day and night shall not cease.

- Genesis 8:22

cease

cease: stop, end

Write the word **cease** and its meaning on the lines below.

_____

_____

_____

_____

_____

While the earth remaineth, seedtime and harvest, and cold and heat, and summer and winter, and day and night shall not cease.

- Genesis 8:22

cease

cease: stop, end

Write the Bible verse from above (Genesis 48:22) on the lines below.

_____

_____

_____

_____

_____

_____

While the earth remaineth, seedtime and harvest, and cold and heat, and summer and winter, and day and night shall not cease.

- Genesis 8:22

cease

cease: stop, end

On the lines below, write your own sentence using the word **cease**.

_____

_____

_____

_____

_____

_____

Hold thou me up, and I shall be safe: and I will have respect unto thy statutes continually.

- Psalm 119:117

safe

<u>safe</u>: out of reach of danger or harm

Write the word **safe** on the line below.

_____

Hold thou me up, and I shall be safe: and I will have respect unto thy statutes continually.

- Psalm 119:117

safe

<u>safe</u>: out of reach of danger or harm

Write the word **safe** on each line below.

_____

_____

_____

Hold thou me up, and I shall be safe: and I will have respect unto thy statutes continually.

- Psalm 119:117

safe

safe: out of reach of danger or harm

Write the word **safe** and its meaning on the lines below.

_____

_____

_____

_____

_____

Hold thou me up, and I shall be safe: and I will have respect unto thy statutes continually.

- Psalm 119:117

safe

safe: out of reach of danger or harm

Write the Bible verse from above (Psalm 119:117) on the lines below.

_____

_____

_____

_____

_____

Hold thou me up, and I shall be safe: and I will have respect unto thy statutes continually.

- Psalm 119:117

safe

safe: out of reach of danger or harm

On the lines below, write your own sentence using the word **safe**.

_____

_____

_____

_____

_____

_____

And he made them a feast, and they did eat and drink.

- Genesis 26:30

feast

feast: a large celebratory meal

Write the word **feast** on the line below.

_____

And he made them a feast, and they did eat and drink.

- Genesis 26:30

feast

feast: a large celebratory meal

Write the word **feast** on each line below.

_____

_____

_____

And he made them a feast, and they did eat and drink.

- Genesis 26:30

feast

feast: a large celebratory meal

Write the word **feast** and its meaning on the lines below.

_____

_____

_____

_____

_____

And he made them a feast, and they did eat and drink.

- Genesis 26:30

feast

feast: a large celebratory meal

Write the Bible verse from above (Genesis 26:30) on the lines below.

_____

_____

_____

_____

_____

_____

And he made them a feast, and they did eat and drink.

- Genesis 26:30

feast

feast: a large celebratory meal

On the lines below, write your own sentence using the word **feast**.

_____

_____

_____

_____

_____

And her gates shall lament and mourn; and she being desolate shall sit upon the ground.

- Isaiah 3:26

lament

lament: feel sorrowful

Write the word **lament** on the line below.

_____

And her gates shall lament and mourn; and she being desolate shall sit upon the ground.

- Isaiah 3:26

lament

lament: feel sorrowful

Write the word **lament** on each line below.

_____

_____

_____

And her gates shall lament and mourn; and she being desolate shall sit upon the ground.

- Isaiah 3:26

lament

lament: feel sorrowful

Write the word **lament** and its meaning on the lines below.

_____

_____

_____

_____

_____

And her gates shall lament and mourn; and she being desolate shall sit upon the ground.

- Isaiah 3:26

lament

lament: feel sorrowful

Write the Bible verse from above (Isaiah 3:26) on the lines below.

_____

_____

_____

_____

_____

_____

And her gates shall lament and mourn; and she being desolate shall sit upon the ground.

- Isaiah 3:26

lament

lament: feel sorrowful

On the lines below, write your own sentence using the word **lament**.

_____

_____

_____

_____

_____

_____

And the Lord shall **sever** between the cattle of Israel and the cattle of Egypt: and there shall nothing die of all that is the children's of Israel.

- Exodus 9:4

sever

sever: separate, divide or cut into separate parts

Write the word **sever** on the line below.

_____

And the Lord shall **sever** between the cattle of Israel and the cattle of Egypt: and there shall nothing die of all that is the children's of Israel.

- Exodus 9:4

sever

sever: separate, divide or cut into separate parts

Write the word **sever** on each line below.

_____

_____

_____

And the Lord shall **sever** between the cattle of Israel and the cattle of Egypt: and there shall nothing die of all that is the children's of Israel.

- Exodus 9:4

sever

sever: separate, divide or cut into separate parts

Write the word **sever** and its meaning on the lines below.

_____

_____

_____

_____

_____

And the Lord shall **sever** between the cattle of Israel and the cattle of Egypt: and there shall nothing die of all that is the children's of Israel.

- Exodus 9:4

sever

sever: separate, divide or cut into separate parts

Write the Bible verse from above (Isaiah 3:26) on the lines below.

_____

_____

_____

_____

_____

_____

And the Lord shall **sever** between the cattle of Israel and the cattle of Egypt: and there shall nothing die of all that is the children's of Israel.

- Exodus 9:4

sever

<u>sever</u>: separate, divide or cut into separate parts

On the lines below, write your own sentence using the word **sever**.

_____

_____

_____

_____

_____

And it came to pass, as they journeyed from the east, that they found a plain in the land of Shinar; and they dwelt there.

- Genesis 11:2

journeyed

journeyed: traveled

Write the word **journeyed** on the line below.

_____

And it came to pass, as they journeyed from the east, that they found a plain in the land of Shinar; and they dwelt there.

- Genesis 11:2

journeyed

journeyed: traveled

Write the word **journeyed** on each line below.

_____

_____

_____

And it came to pass, as they journeyed from the east, that they found a plain in the land of Shinar; and they dwelt there.

- Genesis 11:2

journeyed

journeyed: traveled

Write the word **journeyed** and its meaning on the lines below.

_____

_____

_____

_____

_____

_____

And it came to pass, as they journeyed from the east, that they found a plain in the land of Shinar; and they dwelt there.

- Genesis 11:2

journeyed

journeyed: traveled

Write the Bible verse from above (Genesis 11:2) on the lines below.

_____

_____

_____

_____

_____

And it came to pass, as they journeyed from the east, that they found a plain in the land of Shinar; and they dwelt there.

- Genesis 11:2

journeyed

journeyed: traveled

On the lines below, write your own sentence using the word **journeyed**.

_____

_____

_____

_____

_____

And God blessed Noah and his sons, and said unto them, Be fruitful, and multiply, and replenish the earth.

- Genesis 9:1

replenish

replenish: fill

Write the word **replenish** on the line below.

_____

And God blessed Noah and his sons, and said unto them, Be fruitful, and multiply, and replenish the earth.

- Genesis 9:1

replenish

replenish: fill

Write the word **replenish** on each line below.

_____

_____

_____

And God blessed Noah and his sons, and said unto them, Be fruitful, and multiply, and replenish the earth.

- Genesis 9:1

replenish

replenish: fill

Write the word **replenish** and its meaning on the lines below.

_____

_____

_____

_____

_____

And God blessed Noah and his sons, and said unto them, Be fruitful, and multiply, and replenish the earth.

- Genesis 9:1

replenish

replenish: fill

Write the Bible verse from above (Genesis 9:1) on the lines below.

_____

_____

_____

_____

_____

And God blessed Noah and his sons, and said unto them, Be fruitful, and multiply, and replenish the earth.

- Genesis 9:1

replenish

replenish: fill

On the lines below, write your own sentence using the word **replenish**.

_____

_____

_____

_____

_____

He will not suffer thy foot to be moved: he that keepeth thee will not slumber.

- Psalm 121:3

slumber

slumber: sleep lightly, doze

Write the word **slumber** on the line below.

_____

He will not suffer thy foot to be moved: he that keepeth thee will not slumber.

- Psalm 121:3

slumber

slumber: sleep lightly, doze

Write the word **slumber** on each line below.

_____

_____

_____

He will not suffer thy foot to be moved: he that keepeth thee will not slumber.

- Psalm 121:3

slumber

<u>slumber</u>: sleep lightly, doze

Write the word **slumber** and its meaning on the lines below.

_____

_____

_____

_____

_____

_____

He will not suffer thy foot to be moved: he that keepeth thee will not slumber.

- Psalm 121:3

slumber

slumber: sleep lightly, doze

Write the Bible verse from above (Psalm 121:3) on the lines below.

_____

_____

_____

_____

_____

He will not suffer thy foot to be moved: he that keepeth thee will not slumber.

- Psalm 121:3

slumber

slumber: sleep lightly, doze

On the lines below, write your own sentence using the word **slumber**.

_____

_____

_____

_____

_____

And ye shall observe this thing for an ordinance to thee and to thy sons for ever.

- Exodus 12:24

ordinance

ordinance: a rule established by authority

Write the word **ordinance** on the line below.

_____

And ye shall observe this thing for an ordinance to thee and to thy sons for ever.

- Exodus 12:24

ordinance

ordinance: a rule established by authority

Write the word **ordinance** on each line below.

_____

_____

_____

And ye shall observe this thing for an ordinance to thee and to thy sons for ever.

- Exodus 12:24

ordinance

ordinance: a rule established by authority

Write the word **ordinance** and its meaning on the lines below.

_____

_____

_____

_____

_____

And ye shall observe this thing for an ordinance to thee and to thy sons for ever.

- Exodus 12:24

ordinance

ordinance: a rule established by authority

Write the Bible verse from above (Exodus 12:24) on the lines below.

_____

_____

_____

_____

_____

And ye shall observe this thing for an ordinance to thee and to thy sons for ever.

- Exodus 12:24

ordinance

ordinance: a rule established by authority

On the lines below, write your own sentence using the word **ordinance**.

_____

_____

_____

_____

_____

And as some spake of the temple, how it was adorned with goodly stones and gifts, he said,

- Luke 21:5

adorned

adorned: decorated

Write the word **adorned** on the line below.

_____

And as some spake of the temple, how it was adorned with goodly stones and gifts, he said,

- Luke 21:5

adorned

adorned: decorated

Write the word **adorned** on each line below.

_____

_____

_____

And as some spake of the temple, how it was adorned with goodly stones and gifts, he said,

- Luke 21:5

adorned

adorned: decorated

Write the word **adorned** and its meaning on the lines below.

_____

_____

_____

_____

_____

And as some spake of the temple, how it was adorned with goodly stones and gifts, he said,

- Luke 21:5

adorned

adorned: decorated

Write the Bible verse from above (Luke 21:5) on the lines below.

_____

_____

_____

_____

_____

And as some spake of the temple, how it was adorned with goodly stones and gifts, he said,

- Luke 21:5

adorned

adorned: decorated

On the lines below, write your own sentence using the word **adorned**.

_____

_____

_____

_____

_____

He answereth and saith unto them, He that hath two coats, let him impart to him that hath none; and he that hath meat, let him do likewise.

- Luke 3:11

impart

impart: give

Write the word **impart** on the line below.

_____

He answereth and saith unto them, He that hath two coats, let him impart to him that hath none; and he that hath meat, let him do likewise.

- Luke 3:11

impart

impart: give

Write the word **impart** on each line below.

_____

_____

_____

He answereth and saith unto them, He that hath two coats, let him impart to him that hath none; and he that hath meat, let him do likewise.

- Luke 3:11

impart

impart: give

Write the word **impart** and its meaning on the lines below.

_____

_____

_____

_____

_____

_____

He answereth and saith unto them, He that hath two coats, let him impart to him that hath none; and he that hath meat, let him do likewise.

- Luke 3:11

impart

impart: give

Write the Bible verse from above (Luke 3:11) on the lines below.

_____

_____

_____

_____

_____

He answereth and saith unto them, He that hath two coats, let him impart to him that hath none; and he that hath meat, let him do likewise.

- Luke 3:11

impart

impart: give

On the lines below, write your own sentence using the word **impart**.

_____

_____

_____

_____

_____

And David prepared iron in abundance for the nails for the doors of the gates, and for the joinings; and brass in abundance without weight;

- 1 Chronicles 22:3

abundance

<u>abundance</u>: plenty, an overflowing amount

Write the word **abundance** on the line below.

_____

And David prepared iron in abundance for the nails for the doors of the gates, and for the joinings; and brass in abundance without weight;

- 1 Chronicles 22:3

abundance

abundance: plenty, an overflowing amount

Write the word **abundance** on each line below.

_____

_____

_____

And David prepared iron in abundance for the nails for the doors of the gates, and for the joinings; and brass in abundance without weight;

- 1 Chronicles 22:3

abundance

abundance: plenty, an overflowing amount

Write the word **abundance** and its meaning on the lines below.

_____

_____

_____

_____

_____

_____

And David prepared iron in abundance for the nails for the doors of the gates, and for the joinings; and brass in abundance without weight;

- 1 Chronicles 22:3

abundance

abundance: plenty, an overflowing amount

Write the Bible verse from above (1 Chronicles 22:3) on the lines below.

_____

_____

_____

_____

_____

And David prepared iron in abundance for the nails for the doors of the gates, and for the joinings; and brass in abundance without weight;

- 1 Chronicles 22:3

abundance

abundance: plenty, an overflowing amount

On the lines below, write your own sentence using the word **abundance**.

_____

_____

_____

_____

_____

He will fulfil the desire of them that fear him: he also will hear their cry, and will save them.

- Psalm 145:19

desire

desire: want

Write the word **desire** on the line below.

_____

He will fulfil the desire of them that fear him: he also will hear their cry, and will save them.

- Psalm 145:19

desire

<u>desire</u>: want

Write the word **desire** on each line below.

_____

_____

_____

He will fulfil the desire of them that fear him: he also will hear their cry, and will save them.

- Psalm 145:19

desire

<u>desire</u>: want

Write the word **desire** and its meaning on the lines below.

_____

_____

_____

_____

_____

He will fulfil the desire of them that fear him: he also will hear their cry, and will save them.

- Psalm 145:19

desire

desire: want

Write the Bible verse from above (Psalm 145:19) on the lines below.

_____

_____

_____

_____

_____

He will fulfil the desire of them that fear him: he also will hear their cry, and will save them.

- Psalm 145:19

desire

<u>desire</u>: want

On the lines below, write your own sentence using the word **desire**.

_____

_____

_____

_____

_____

Thou shalt not curse the deaf, nor put a stumblingblock before the blind, but shalt fear thy God: I am the Lord.

- Leviticus 19:14

curse

curse: say you wish something evil to happen to someone

Write the word **curse** on the line below.

_____

Thou shalt not curse the deaf, nor put a stumblingblock before the blind, but shalt fear thy God: I am the Lord.

- Leviticus 19:14

curse

curse: say you wish something evil to happen to someone

Write the word **curse** on each line below.

_____

_____

_____

Thou shalt not curse the deaf, nor put a stumblingblock before the blind, but shalt fear thy God: I am the Lord.

- Leviticus 19:14

curse

curse: say you wish something evil to happen to someone

Write the word **curse** and its meaning on the lines below.

_____

_____

_____

_____

_____

_____

Thou shalt not curse the deaf, nor put a stumblingblock before the blind, but shalt fear thy God: I am the Lord.

- Leviticus 19:14

curse

curse: say you wish something evil to happen to someone

Write the Bible verse from above (Leviticus 19:14) on the lines below.

_____

_____

_____

_____

_____

Thou shalt not curse the deaf, nor put a stumblingblock before the blind, but shalt fear thy God: I am the Lord.

- Leviticus 19:14

curse

<u>curse</u>: say you wish something evil to happen to someone

On the lines below, write your own sentence using the word **curse**.

_____

_____

_____

_____

_____

The oath which he sware to our father Abraham,

- Luke 1:73

oath

oath: a promise

Write the word **oath** on the line below.

_____

The oath which he sware to our father Abraham,

- Luke 1:73

oath

oath: a promise

Write the word **oath** on each line below.

_____

_____

_____

The oath which he sware to our father Abraham,

- Luke 1:73

oath

oath: a promise

Write the word **oath** and its meaning on the lines below.

_____

_____

_____

_____

_____

The oath which he sware to our father Abraham,

- Luke 1:73

oath

oath: a promise

Write the Bible verse from above (Luke 1:73) on the lines below.

_____

_____

_____

_____

_____

The oath which he sware to our father Abraham,

- Luke 1:73

oath

oath: a promise

On the lines below, write your own sentence using the word **oath**.

_____

_____

_____

_____

_____

And the fish that is in the river shall die, and the river shall stink; and the Egyptians shall lothe to drink of the water of the river.

- Exodus 7:18

lothe

lothe: hate

Write the word **lothe** on the line below.

_____

And the fish that is in the river shall die, and the river shall stink; and the Egyptians shall lothe to drink of the water of the river.

- Exodus 7:18

lothe

lothe: hate

Write the word **lothe** on each line below.

_____

_____

_____

And the fish that is in the river shall die, and the river shall stink; and the Egyptians shall lothe to drink of the water of the river.

- Exodus 7:18

lothe

lothe: hate

Write the word **lothe** and its meaning on the lines below.

_____

_____

_____

_____

_____

_____

And the fish that is in the river shall die, and the river shall stink; and the Egyptians shall lothe to drink of the water of the river.

- Exodus 7:18

lothe

lothe: hate

Write the Bible verse from above (Exodus 7:18) on the lines below.

_____

_____

_____

_____

_____

And the fish that is in the river shall die, and the river shall stink; and the Egyptians shall lothe to drink of the water of the river.

- Exodus 7:18

lothe

lothe: hate

On the lines below, write your own sentence using the word **lothe**.

_____

_____

_____

_____

_____

A false witness that speaketh lies, and he that soweth discord among brethren.

- Proverbs 6:19

discord

discord: disagreement

Write the word **discord** on the line below.

_____

A false witness that speaketh lies, and he that soweth discord among brethren.

- Proverbs 6:19

discord

discord: disagreement

Write the word **discord** on each line below.

_____

_____

_____

A false witness that speaketh lies, and he that soweth discord among brethren.

- Proverbs 6:19

discord

discord: disagreement

Write the word **discord** and its meaning on the lines below.

_____

_____

_____

_____

_____

A false witness that speaketh lies, and he that soweth discord among brethren.

- Proverbs 6:19

discord

discord: disagreement

Write the Bible verse from above (Proverbs 6:19) on the lines below.

_____

_____

_____

_____

_____

_____

A false witness that speaketh lies, and he that soweth discord among brethren.

- Proverbs 6:19

discord

discord: disagreement

On the lines below, write your own sentence using the word **discord**.

_____

_____

_____

_____

_____

And I will make my covenant between me and thee, and will multiply thee exceedingly.

- Genesis 17:2

covenant

covenant: agreement

Write the word **covenant** on the line below.

_____

And I will make my covenant between me and thee, and will multiply thee exceedingly.

- Genesis 17:2

covenant

<u>covenant</u>: agreement

Write the word **covenant** on each line below.

_____

_____

_____

And I will make my covenant between me and thee, and will multiply thee exceedingly.

- Genesis 17:2

covenant

covenant: agreement

Write the word **covenant** and its meaning on the lines below.

_____

_____

_____

_____

_____

And I will make my covenant between me and thee, and will multiply thee exceedingly.

- Genesis 17:2

covenant

covenant: agreement

Write the Bible verse from above (Genesis 17:2) on the lines below.

_____

_____

_____

_____

_____

And I will make my covenant between me and thee, and will multiply thee exceedingly.

- Genesis 17:2

covenant

covenant: agreement

On the lines below, write your own sentence using the word **covenant**.

_____

_____

_____

_____

_____

He that sacrificeth unto any god, save unto the Lord only, he shall be utterly destroyed.

- Exodus 22:20

utterly

<u>utterly</u>: completely

Write the word **utterly** on the line below.

_____

He that sacrificeth unto any god, save unto the Lord only, he shall be utterly destroyed.

- Exodus 22:20

utterly

<u>utterly</u>: completely

Write the word **utterly** on each line below.

_____

_____

_____

He that sacrificeth unto any god, save unto the Lord only, he shall be utterly destroyed.

- Exodus 22:20

utterly

<u>utterly</u>: completely

Write the word **utterly** and its meaning on the lines below.

_____

_____

_____

_____

_____

He that sacrificeth unto any god, save unto the Lord only, he shall be utterly destroyed.

- Exodus 22:20

utterly

utterly: completely

Write the Bible verse from above (Exodus 22:20) on the lines below.

_____

_____

_____

_____

_____

He that sacrificeth unto any god, save unto the Lord only, he shall be utterly destroyed.

- Exodus 22:20

utterly

utterly: completely

On the lines below, write your own sentence using the word **utterly**.

_____

_____

_____

_____

_____

Now therefore, I pray thee, pardon my sin, and turn again with me, that I may worship the LORD.

- 1 Samuel 15:25

pardon

pardon: forgive, excuse

Write the word **pardon** on the line below.

_____

Now therefore, I pray thee, pardon my sin, and turn again with me, that I may worship the LORD.

- 1 Samuel 15:25

pardon

pardon: forgive, excuse

Write the word **pardon** on each line below.

_____

_____

_____

Now therefore, I pray thee, pardon my sin, and turn again with me, that I may worship the LORD.

- 1 Samuel 15:25

pardon

pardon: forgive, excuse

Write the word **pardon** and its meaning on the lines below.

_____

_____

_____

_____

_____

_____

Now therefore, I pray thee, pardon my sin, and turn again with me, that I may worship the LORD.

- 1 Samuel 15:25

pardon

pardon: forgive, excuse

Write the Bible verse from above (1 Samuel 15:25) on the lines below.

_____

_____

_____

_____

_____

_____

Now therefore, I pray thee, pardon my sin, and turn again with me, that I may worship the LORD.

- 1 Samuel 15:25

pardon

pardon: forgive, excuse

On the lines below, write your own sentence using the word **pardon**.

_____

_____

_____

_____

_____

_____

Verily, verily, I say unto you, He that believeth on me hath everlasting life.

- John 6:47

everlasting

everlasting: lasting forever, without end, eternal

Write the word **everlasting** on the line below.

_____

Verily, verily, I say unto you, He that believeth on me hath everlasting life.

- John 6:47

everlasting

everlasting: lasting forever, without end, eternal

Write the word **everlasting** on each line below.

_____

_____

_____

Verily, verily, I say unto you, He that believeth on me hath everlasting life.

- John 6:47

everlasting

everlasting: lasting forever, without end, eternal

Write the word **everlasting** and its meaning on the lines below.

_____

_____

_____

_____

_____

Verily, verily, I say unto you, He that believeth on me hath everlasting life.

- John 6:47

everlasting

everlasting: lasting forever, without end, eternal

Write the Bible verse from above (John 6:47) on the lines below.

_____

_____

_____

_____

_____

_____

Verily, verily, I say unto you, He that believeth on me hath everlasting life.

- John 6:47

everlasting

everlasting: lasting forever, without end, eternal

On the lines below, write your own sentence using the word **everlasting**.

_____

_____

_____

_____

_____

Trust in the LORD, and do good; so shalt thou dwell in the land, and verily thou shalt be fed.

- Psalm 37:3

verily

verily: certainly, truly, really, in fact

Write the word **verily** on the line below.

_____

Trust in the L ORD , and do good; so shalt thou dwell in the land, and verily thou shalt be fed.

- Psalm 37:3

verily

verily: certainly, truly, really, in fact

Write the word **verily** on each line below.

_____

_____

_____

Trust in the LORD, and do good; so shalt thou dwell in the land, and verily thou shalt be fed.

- Psalm 37:3

verily

verily: certainly, truly, really, in fact

Write the word **verily** and its meaning on the lines below.

_____

_____

_____

_____

_____

_____

Trust in the LORD, and do good; so shalt thou dwell in the land, and verily thou shalt be fed.

- Psalm 37:3

verily

verily: certainly, truly, really, in fact

Write the Bible verse from above (Psalm 37:3) on the lines below.

_____

_____

_____

_____

_____

Trust in the LORD, and do good; so shalt thou dwell in the land, and verily thou shalt be fed.

- Psalm 37:3

verily

verily: certainly, truly, really, in fact

On the lines below, write your own sentence using the word **verily**.

_____

_____

_____

_____

_____

I beheld the transgressors, and was grieved; because they kept not thy word.

- Psalm 119:158

transgressors

transgressors: law breakers, sinners

Write the word **transgressors** on the line below.

_____

I beheld the transgressors, and was grieved; because they kept not thy word.

- Psalm 119:158

transgressors

transgressors: law breakers, sinners

Write the word **transgressors** on each line below.

_____

_____

_____

I beheld the transgressors, and was grieved; because they kept not thy word.

- Psalm 119:158

transgressors

transgressors: law breakers, sinners

Write the word **transgressors** and its meaning on the lines below.

_____

_____

_____

_____

_____

_____

I beheld the transgressors, and was grieved; because they kept not thy word.

- Psalm 119:158

transgressors

transgressors: law breakers, sinners

Write the Bible verse from above (Psalm 119:158) on the lines below.

_____

_____

_____

_____

_____

_____

I beheld the transgressors, and was grieved; because they kept not thy word.

- Psalm 119:158

transgressors

transgressors: law breakers, sinners

On the lines below, write your own sentence using the word **transgressors**.

_____

_____

_____

_____

_____

If thy brother be waxen poor, and hath sold away some of his possession, and if any of his kin come to redeem it, then shall he redeem that which his brother sold.

- Leviticus 25:25

kin

kin: relatives

Write the word **kin** on the line below.

_____

If thy brother be waxen poor, and hath sold away some of his possession, and if any of his kin come to redeem it, then shall he redeem that which his brother sold.

- Leviticus 25:25

kin

kin: relatives

Write the word **kin** on each line below.

_____

_____

_____

If thy brother be waxen poor, and hath sold away some of his possession, and if any of his kin come to redeem it, then shall he redeem that which his brother sold.

- Leviticus 25:25

kin

kin: relatives

Write the word **kin** and its meaning on the lines below.

_____

_____

_____

_____

_____

If thy brother be waxen poor, and hath sold away some of his possession, and if any of his kin come to redeem it, then shall he redeem that which his brother sold.

- Leviticus 25:25

kin

kin: relatives

Write the Bible verse from above (Leviticus 25:25) on the lines below.

_____

_____

_____

_____

_____

If thy brother be waxen poor, and hath sold away some of his possession, and if any of his kin come to redeem it, then shall he redeem that which his brother sold.

- Leviticus 25:25

kin

kin: relatives

On the lines below, write your own sentence using the word **kin**.

_____

_____

_____

_____

_____

_____

Now learn a parable of the fig tree; When his branch is yet tender, and putteth forth leaves, ye know that summer is nigh:

- Matthew 24:32

nigh

nigh: near, close

Write the word **nigh** on the line below.

_____

Now learn a parable of the fig tree; When his branch is yet tender, and putteth forth leaves, ye know that summer is nigh:

- Matthew 24:32

nigh

nigh: near, close

Write the word **nigh** on each line below.

_____

_____

_____

Now learn a parable of the fig tree; When his branch is yet tender, and putteth forth leaves, ye know that summer is nigh:

- Matthew 24:32

nigh

nigh: near, close

Write the word **nigh** and its meaning on the lines below.

_____

_____

_____

_____

_____

Now learn a parable of the fig tree; When his branch is yet tender, and putteth forth leaves, ye know that summer is nigh:

- Matthew 24:32

nigh

nigh: near, close

Write the Bible verse from above (Matthew 24:32) on the lines below.

_____

_____

_____

_____

_____

Now learn a parable of the fig tree; When his branch is yet tender, and putteth forth leaves, ye know that summer is nigh:

- Matthew 24:32

nigh

nigh: near, close

On the lines below, write your own sentence using the word **nigh**.

_____

_____

_____

_____

_____

The LORD is nigh unto them that are of a broken heart; and saveth such as be of a contrite spirit.

- Psalm 34:18

contrite

contrite: sorrowful, humble

Write the word **contrite** on the line below.

_____

The LORD is nigh unto them that are of a broken heart; and saveth such as be of a contrite spirit.

- Psalm 34:18

contrite

contrite: sorrowful, humble

Write the word **contrite** on each line below.

_____

_____

_____

The LORD is nigh unto them that are of a broken heart; and saveth such as be of a contrite spirit.

- Psalm 34:18

contrite

contrite: sorrowful, humble

Write the word **contrite** and its meaning on the lines below.

_____

_____

_____

_____

_____

_____

The LORD is nigh unto them that are of a broken heart; and saveth such as be of a contrite spirit.

- Psalm 34:18

contrite

<u>contrite</u>: sorrowful, humble

Write the Bible verse from above (Psalm 34:18) on the lines below.

_____

_____

_____

_____

_____

The LORD is nigh unto them that are of a broken heart; and saveth such as be of a contrite spirit.

- Psalm 34:18

contrite

contrite: sorrowful, humble

On the lines below, write your own sentence using the word **contrite**.

_____

_____

_____

_____

_____

_____

Woe unto you, scribes and Pharisees, hypocrites! for ye pay tithe of mint and anise and cummin, and have omitted the weightier matters of the law, judgment, mercy, and faith: these ought ye to have done, and not to leave the other undone.

- Matthew 23:23

omitted

omitted: left out

Write the word **omitted** on the line below.

_____

Woe unto you, scribes and Pharisees, hypocrites! for ye pay tithe of mint and anise and cummin, and have omitted the weightier matters of the law, judgment, mercy, and faith: these ought ye to have done, and not to leave the other undone.

- Matthew 23:23

omitted

omitted: left out

Write the word **omitted** on each line below.

_____

_____

_____

Woe unto you, scribes and Pharisees, hypocrites! for ye pay tithe of mint and anise and cummin, and have omitted the weightier matters of the law, judgment, mercy, and faith: these ought ye to have done, and not to leave the other undone.

- Matthew 23:23

omitted

omitted: left out

Write the word **omitted** and its meaning on the lines below.

_____

_____

_____

_____

_____

Woe unto you, scribes and Pharisees, hypocrites! for ye pay tithe of mint and anise and cummin, and have omitted the weightier matters of the law, judgment, mercy, and faith: these ought ye to have done, and not to leave the other undone.   - Matthew 23:23

omitted

omitted: left out

Write the first through third lines of the Bible verse from above (Matthew 23:23) on the lines below.

_____

_____

_____

_____

_____

_____

Woe unto you, scribes and Pharisees, hypocrites! for ye pay tithe of mint and anise and cummin, and have omitted the weightier matters of the law, judgment, mercy, and faith: these ought ye to have done, and not to leave the other undone.

- Matthew 23:23

omitted

omitted: left out

On the lines below, write your own sentence using the word **omittted**.

_____

_____

_____

_____

_____

Speaking to yourselves in psalms and hymns and spiritual songs, singing and making melody in your heart to the Lord;

- Ephesians 5:19

melody

melody: music, song

Write the word **melody** on the line below.

_____

Speaking to yourselves in psalms and hymns and spiritual songs, singing and making melody in your heart to the Lord;

- Ephesians 5:19

melody

melody: music, song

Write the word **melody** on each line below.

_____

_____

_____

Speaking to yourselves in psalms and hymns and spiritual songs, singing and making melody in your heart to the Lord;

- Ephesians 5:19

melody

melody: music, song

Write the word **melody** and its meaning on the lines below.

_____

_____

_____

_____

_____

_____

Speaking to yourselves in psalms and hymns and spiritual songs, singing and making melody in your heart to the Lord;

- Ephesians 5:19

melody

melody: music, song

Write the Bible verse from above (Ephesians 5:19) on the lines below.

_____

_____

_____

_____

_____

Speaking to yourselves in psalms and hymns and spiritual songs, singing and making melody in your heart to the Lord;

- Ephesians 5:19

melody

melody: music, song

On the lines below, write your own sentence using the word **melody**.

_____

_____

_____

_____

_____

Then came his disciples, and said unto him, Knowest thou that the Pharisees were offended, after they heard this saying?

- Matthew 15:12

offended

offended: displeased

Write the word **offended** on the line below.

_____

Then came his disciples, and said unto him, Knowest thou that the Pharisees were offended, after they heard this saying?

- Matthew 15:12

offended

offended: displeased

Write the word **offended** on each line below.

_____

_____

_____

Then came his disciples, and said unto him, Knowest thou that the Pharisees were offended, after they heard this saying?

- Matthew 15:12

offended

offended: displeased

Write the word **offended** and its meaning on the lines below.

_____

_____

_____

_____

_____

_____

Then came his disciples, and said unto him, Knowest thou that the Pharisees were offended, after they heard this saying?

- Matthew 15:12

offended

offended: displeased

Write the Bible verse from above (Matthew 15:12) on the lines below.

_____

_____

_____

_____

_____

Then came his disciples, and said unto him, Knowest thou that the Pharisees were offended, after they heard this saying?

- Matthew 15:12

offended

offended: displeased

On the lines below, write your own sentence using the word **offended**.

_____

_____

_____

_____

_____

This he said, not that he cared for the poor; but because he was a thief, and had the bag, and bare what was put therein.

- John 12:6

thief

thief: someone who steals

Write the word **thief** on the line below.

_____

This he said, not that he cared for the poor; but because he was a thief, and had the bag, and bare what was put therein.

- John 12:6

thief

thief: someone who steals

Write the word **thief** on each line below.

_____

_____

_____

This he said, not that he cared for the poor; but because he was a thief, and had the bag, and bare what was put therein.

- John 12:6

thief

thief: someone who steals

Write the word **thief** and its meaning on the lines below.

_____

_____

_____

_____

_____

_____

This he said, not that he cared for the poor; but because he was a thief, and had the bag, and bare what was put therein.

- John 12:6

thief

thief: someone who steals

Write the Bible verse from above John 12:6) on the lines below.

_____

_____

_____

_____

_____

This he said, not that he cared for the poor; but because he was a thief, and had the bag, and bare what was put therein.

- John 12:6

thief

thief: someone who steals

On the lines below, write your own sentence using the word **thief**.

_____

_____

_____

_____

_____

_____

But now the Lord my God hath given me rest on every side, so that there is neither adversary nor evil occurrent.

- 1 Kings 5:4

adversary

adversary: enemy, foe

Write the word **adversary** on the line below.

_____

But now the Lord my God hath given me rest on every side, so that there is neither adversary nor evil occurrent.

- 1 Kings 5:4

adversary

adversary: enemy, foe

Write the word **adversary** on each line below.

_____

_____

_____

But now the Lord my God hath given me rest on every side, so that there is neither adversary nor evil occurrent.

- 1 Kings 5:4

adversary

adversary: enemy, foe

Write the word **adversary** and its meaning on the lines below.

_____

_____

_____

_____

_____

_____

But now the Lord my God hath given me rest on every side, so that there is neither adversary nor evil occurrent.

- 1 Kings 5:4

adversary

adversary: enemy, foe

Write the Bible verse from above (1 Kings 5:4) on the lines below.

_____

_____

_____

_____

_____

But now the Lord my God hath given me rest on every side, so that there is neither adversary nor evil occurrent.

- 1 Kings 5:4

adversary

adversary: enemy, foe

On the lines below, write your own sentence using the word **adversary**.

_____

_____

_____

_____

_____

_____

Now unto the King eternal, immortal, invisible, the only wise God, be honour and glory for ever and ever. Amen.

- 1 Timothy 1:17

immortal

immortal: never ending, everlasting, exempt from death

Write the word **immortal** on the line below.

_____

Now unto the King eternal, immortal, invisible, the only wise God, be honour and glory for ever and ever. Amen.

- 1 Timothy 1:17

immortal

immortal: never ending, everlasting, exempt from death

Write the word **immortal** on each line below.

_____

_____

_____

Now unto the King eternal, immortal, invisible, the only wise God, be honour and glory for ever and ever. Amen.

- 1 Timothy 1:17

immortal

immortal: never ending, everlasting, exempt from death

Write the word **immortal** and its meaning on the lines below.

_____

_____

_____

_____

_____

Now unto the King eternal, immortal, invisible, the only wise God, be honour and glory for ever and ever. Amen.

- 1 Timothy 1:17

immortal

immortal: never ending, everlasting, exempt from death

Write the Bible verse from above (1 Timothy 1:17) on the lines below.

_____

_____

_____

_____

_____

Now unto the King eternal, immortal, invisible, the only wise God, be honour and glory for ever and ever. Amen.

- 1 Timothy 1:17

immortal

immortal: never ending, everlasting, exempt from death

On the lines below, write your own sentence using the word **immortal**.

_____

_____

_____

_____

_____

They are passed away as the swift ships: as the eagle that hasteth to the prey.

- Job 9:26

swift

<u>swift</u>: quick, speedy, prompt, fast, without delay

Write the word **swift** on the line below.

_____

They are passed away as the swift ships: as the eagle that hasteth to the prey.

- Job 9:26

swift

swift: quick, speedy, prompt, fast, without delay

Write the word **swift** on each line below.

_____

_____

_____

They are passed away as the swift ships: as the eagle that hasteth to the prey.

- Job 9:26

swift

swift: quick, speedy, prompt, fast, without delay

Write the word **swift** and its meaning on the lines below.

_____

_____

_____

_____

_____

_____

They are passed away as the swift ships: as the eagle that hasteth to the prey.

- Job 9:26

swift

swift: quick, speedy, prompt, fast, without delay

Write the Bible verse from above (Job 9:26) on the lines below.

_____

_____

_____

_____

_____

They are passed away as the swift ships: as the eagle that hasteth to the prey.

- Job 9:26

swift

swift: quick, speedy, prompt, fast, without delay

On the lines below, write your own sentence using the word **swift**.

_____

_____

_____

_____

_____

And there was delivered unto him the book of the prophet Esaias. And when he had opened the book, he found the place where it was written,

- Luke 4:17

prophet

prophet: someone inspired or instructed by God to announce future events

Write the word **prophet** on the line below.

_____

And there was delivered unto him the book of the prophet Esaias. And when he had opened the book, he found the place where it was written,

- Luke 4:17

prophet

prophet: someone inspired or instructed by God to announce future events

Write the word **prophet** on each line below.

_____

_____

_____

And there was delivered unto him the book of the prophet Esaias. And when he had opened the book, he found the place where it was written,

- Luke 4:17

prophet

prophet: someone inspired or instructed by God to announce future events

Write the word **prophet** and its meaning on the lines below.

_____

_____

_____

_____

_____

_____

And there was delivered unto him the book of the prophet Esaias. And when he had opened the book, he found the place where it was written,

- Luke 4:17

prophet

prophet: someone inspired or instructed by God to announce future events

Write the Bible verse from above (Luke 4:17) on the lines below.

_____

_____

_____

_____

_____

And there was delivered unto him the book of the prophet Esaias. And when he had opened the book, he found the place where it was written,

- Luke 4:17

prophet

prophet: someone inspired or instructed by God to announce future events

On the lines below, write your own sentence using the word **prophet**.

_____

_____

_____

_____

_____

Notes

Notes

Notes

Notes

To purchase additional copies of this book, or to purchase copies of any other books by Randi, search for Randi Millward on Amazon.com, or contact your local bookstore.

For whosoever shall call upon the name of the Lord shall be saved.

Romans 10:13

www.ingramcontent.com/pod-product-compliance
Lightning Source LLC
Chambersburg PA
CBHW081212020426

42331CB00012B/2996